Article Marketing

Dominator

The Essential Guide to Maximize Your Online Business Exposure Through the Expert Use of Article Marketing

STEVEN LEE

Table of Contents

The Importance of Article Marketing

Article marketing has been used for years. From media publications, it has shifted to the web which many experts say is timeless thus making it very important in the digital age.

The reason why article marketing is so important is that it will not only enhance your website with information, but it will also make it go up the ranks of major search engines which all boils down to quality traffic. This means that chances of people buying your items via the web are much higher and some of these customers might even come from out of state or from a different country.

A. You can make this happen simply by choosing the right keywords which the search engines will pick up when someone decides to look for it.

B. Another option is to send your articles only to those cater to it. This can be done by uploading article to your favourite online network. There are also popular article submission sites also known as directories as well as article search engines which you can submit to free of charge.

C. You can also get help from friends who also have websites and also post your articles there. The more sites you are able to advertise in better, so you get to reach a larger audience.

D. If you have written a lot of articles already, it is time to put these into categories. You can also put these all together in the form of an e-Book and give this away for free.

E. Articles may be submitted to ezine sites. Article marketing is just one of the tools in promoting your site via web. There are also meta-tags and pop-up tags which happen to be very popular. The only difference is that you have to spend a few dollars in order for these to be posted in other sites.

So, is article marketing important? The answer is yes because with 300 to 500 words, you are able to talk to the reader in a more personal level better than what a banner can do.

Most people do not even pay attention to a banner and just close it because many feels it is a waste of time just entertaining it. Perhaps the best part is that you do not have to be an expert writer to tell the reader what your product is all about. The main thing is that you are able to say it simply so this will be easy for just about anyone to understand.

If you are having a hard time putting words together, do drafts, proofread it before submitting this online. For those who do not write very well, maybe you should hire someone to do that for you by simply giving them certain guidelines about the message you are trying to convey.

People who want to search for something using the web have to type in certain keywords in one of the major search engines.

If you want people to find your site, you have to put yourself in their shoes, then put in factual information so you can be trusted.

This is the essence of what makes article marketing is all about and why it is so important for anyone who wants to do business online.

Some Effective Article Marketing Tips

Article marketing can do a lot for your business.

You just have to know a few things, here are some tips to help you out vital age.

1. First, you have to make sure that whatever you are writing about is relevant. If you know for a fact that your product could be very useful, then do some research about it and then end the article with a link to your website. Before you upload the article, check if the site you plan to put this has this as one of their topics.

2. Just like what you read in the newspaper or see on television, the article must be both timely and newsworthy. This allow you stay in touch with what is happening in the world. One good way is signing up with a site gives you alerts with regards to certain topics.

Some writers post one article and that is it. Just like the movie producers in Hollywood, you should post a sequel to this; there could already be new information available which you could share to the public.

3. You should also make your articles viral. What this simply means is allowing other people to publish your article just as long as nothing is changed, you are given credit for it. Another way of doing this is offering writing services to others which will become added revenue for you.

4. Each article you write must be short, simple. It must be short so that it will not bore reader. Simple so that they will be able to understand the message you are trying to convey.

5. Just how many articles have you to write to increase the traffic? The good news is that you only need 2 to get things started. A good title will be "how to do something" and "x number of tips for something." If this catches their

interest, that person will most likely click on the link to your site and then buy something. The bottom line is that it increases web traffic.

6. You can stop at just 2 articles to promote your site. If you have other products, you can write articles on it as well and then mention in the resource box. This is known as cross-referencing which a lot of webmasters allow their contributors to do.

7. Aside from posting your written work in other websites, do not forget to also put these in your own. If you have written 10 or more about the same topic, put these together to what is known as an e-book and then pass this along for free. Again, if people like what is written there then people would not remind reading it several times.

8. Aside from posting in websites, make use of RSS feeds. There are plenty of them around so make use of it. There are two ways to get into article marketing. The first is to write it

yourself and just hope people appreciate your writing style. The other is to hire someone to do it.

Some charge by the hour while others charge per word. It may be worth it if this increases traffic to your site. By following these article marketing tips, it will not be long before you get a lot of hits.

Writing Easy to Read Articles

When you are writing articles, make sure to keep your readers in mind. Studies have shown most Internet readers tend to scan a page to find what they are looking for, rather than reading the entire page. This means having good titles, subtitles, and making use of bullet points to help your readers easily scan your page. Readers prefer a site easy to use and will be more willing to come back to your site time and time again.

The more that your readers return, the more opportunities you will have to get them to click on each one of your affiliate links. Failing to write your articles, or to have them written this way, could turn your site visitors away before they even have a chance to see what you have to say or to learn what your affiliate links are all about.

Keeping your articles organized as recommended will keep your visitors returning and enable your site to continue making money for you.

Writing Articles About Internet Marketing

Going over an article on Internet marketing, you will gauge how the term has changed through the years. It used to be focused on ad placements.

The way to do it then was to create a web page and place banner ads on other sites so that you can have links to your own sites.

There are also some money-making schemes that evolved wherein you are advised to join a program for you to earn through the Internet.

But as of today, the Internet marketing has become synonymous to advertising. And the best way to do this is through creating valuable articles. This way, it is less costly especially if you have the knack for writing, you are creating your own materials.

Writing the Articles

Writing for the web is a lot different as compared to feature writing on magazines or in newspapers. This can be easy to do once you get the hang of it. All you have got to have are ideas about a specific topic that you want to become an expert on. But if you really do not have the knack for this craft, you can always hire freelancers to do the task for you.

First thing that you have to remember when writing the articles is that you must have a specific audience in mind. You will address your materials to them. You are vying for their attention that is why you are writing your articles in a way to reach out to them.

This is the kind of topics which they are interested to, so you write about it until you are considered and expert. That will not be hard to do especially when you have good content which your target market is always on the lookout for.

You have to be subtle in promoting your own web site, products, and services. This rule applies when you get articles published on different submission sites. Most of the time, you will be allotted a box, an ample space wherein you can create an author's bio. That is the part where you can have a link to your site. The idea here is when you already got the trust of your readers, they will be interested enough to click on your specified links.

Take note of word count. Other submission sites would accept 300 or so words for articles. But most sites prefer 500 to 550 minimum word count. Read the rules thoroughly so that you will not get banned from any of those useful sites.

Also be careful in using keywords. Do not use it too much to the point that it will annoy your readers. Stuffing your articles with keywords will just make your readers turn away from materials as long as your motives become very obvious.

Lastly, choose an article submission site that ranks high on Google and in Alexa. You do not want to submit your work on spammy sites. That will not do your business any good. You can also study where your competitors do their submissions. This way, you can zoom in on those sites and start on your submissions.

Read through an article on Internet marketing just like this one before you plunge into the territory which is still unknown to you.

This way, once you have entered the battle, there will be no turning back.

Using Article Marketing to Help Your Business

Can article marketing help your business? The answer is yes because not only are you able to post your articles for free, but you get to reach a specific audience is interested in your product or service. Article marketing can help your business the minute you submit these to different article directories.

If these are approved for posting, people will be able to visit your site or may want to get in touch with you as they click the link or look at the resource box.

The resource box is usually found at the bottom of the web page. Here, writers can put their name, website, and email. If your article had a significant impact on the reader and they would like to post your article in their websites, they can do so which means more people will be able to see your work without you having to do anything.

Articles that are posted in directories usually ask you for keywords so this can easily be found when someone visits the site. These keywords are also given to search engines so if people type it in, your article will also appear, and they will be able to view it. Another way of getting people to see your site is giving this in the form of a report or e-book to potential customers. With all the information there, that person will surely want to know more and get in touch with you in the future.

People who are serious about the article marketing have to venues where the articles can be displayed.

The first is high traffic distribution sites while the second is submitted to highly relevant niche publishers. The difference between the two is that although the second will not be read by many, it will be easy for those who run this site to refer qualified visitors to the author.

It does not matter if the article you are writing about is for a small, medium, or a large business because there are ways to promote it. For instance, if your article is for a small restaurant, you should put in the title something related to the location of the establishment.

The same goes for the medium and large-scale business. The key here is to come up with a catchy title that your audience can relate to. Of course, there are other ways of promoting your business such as paying for pop up ads and meta-tags. But why would you spend when you can get this for free? So, take advantage of this free marketing tool and see what it can do as it has done for others.

You surely would not want to pass up on the chance so write something about your business or get someone to do it for you. Is article marketing better than conventional print publications? The answer is yes because people will easily find your article by typing in some keywords.

But print publication is difficult because you will have to browse through how many back issues of newspapers and magazines just to find it.

Also, conventional publication is only relevant to the time it was written. The online form will be there for many years ahead as this information is stored somewhere in the cyber space. Just make sure this is updated if something new comes along so you are sure that article marketing is able to help your business.

Writing Great Articles

Article marketing is the new way to promote products nowadays. After all, what better way to reach the target market than to produce materials that directly affect them and articles that they can directly relate with.

For instance, if you have a product that treats diabetes, one way to reach your market and reach your target audience is to write articles that will benefit them like tips on how to prevent increase in sugar levels.

This is especially true with the range that the world wide web has brought us. With the faster connection and the amount of information that one can get with a single click of the mouse, more and more people are starting to recognize importance that article marketing in raising the awareness of consumers.

In recent years that article marketing has gone online, it has not only been used to promote products and services over the internet but also in promotion of the site itself.

Site owners use the articles that they have in their sites to increase their ranking in search engines like Yahoo and Google. The more articles they have that correspond to the keyword being searched on, the better their ranking will be in search results.

This is done not only to increase the viewers that will be able to look at the sites but also the advertisements that will be placed on the site.

More viewers and visitors of the sites will also mean more advertisements on the sites. This will mean more revenues for the site as they get a percentage for every person who will click on the advertisements. But the proliferation of articles on the internet has lowered the quality of the posted works. More and more articles are being posted without proper editing.

There are many articles that have wrong spelling and wrong grammar. There are also a lot of articles that have been copied from other sites. Some will be copied verbatim while other articles will only get the essence of the piece.

But you do not have to sacrifice quality over quantity. Even with a lot of articles to do, you can create great articles. Here are some tips on how to do it.

1. Write as if you are talking to your readers

The best way to make articles easy to read is to make it conversational. Write them in such a way that you talking to your readers. This way, they will be able to relate more with the article and absorb the piece.

2. Use simple words

There is no sense in using words that can only be found in dictionary. After all your readers are not scholars who have a wide vocabulary.

Articles that use complicated words are also boring to read, hard to understand. By using simple words, you can create connection with your readers right there and then. That way, you will be able to accomplish what you came out to do, inform readers and promote your product and site. Besides, if they did not like article, will they be coming back to your site?

3. Write short articles

You are not writing a novel. With online content, shorter is better as most people who use the net will have really short attention spans. They will not have the time or the patience to weed through the additional words that you added just to lengthen the article. As much as possible, make short succinct articles that go straight to the point.

What to Do With Articles You Write

Do enjoy writing articles for your website or blog? If so, did you know that you can use those articles as a way to make money? You can. In fact, you may be surprised just how many options you have. So, what can you do with articles you wrote? Honestly, you can do whatever you want with them. Why?

Because you authored the articles yourself, making you the legal owner. If you opt for outsourcing, make sure you get exclusive rights. Despite the fact that you have freedom in deciding how you want to use your articles, continue reading on for a few helpful tips. If you are a website owner and have a published website, add these articles to that site. This is recommended if you ordered/wrote articles that are similar to your website's main themes. Although any type of article will do, the keyword articles are recommended.

They get picked up by the search engines. This means that you may find your website appearing on front page of Google with applicable internet searches. Articles that you wrote can also be used on a blog. What is nice about this approach is that blog postings are not always expected to be long.

In fact, some readers prefer blog posts that are around 200 to 300 words each. Many like to read blogs that get right to the point. This means that you can divide a longer article into two separate blog postings. Articles can also be submitted to article directories. Unfortunately, this option is often bypassed, as some do not see it as a way to make money.

Do not make the same mistake. When you submit an article to a directory, you get to include a link to your website or blog. Other internet users can post your article on their website, provided your links are still attached. This is an easy way to spread the word and increase your website or blog traffic. Remember the more traffic you receive, the more you are likely to make money. Articles can also be added to revenue sharing websites. These are websites where you are paid for displaying your article online. You may receive a percentage of sales generated through advertisement clicks or affiliate purchases, but you may also receive a set page view bonus.

This approach is not always the first that comes to mind, but you can utilize it. Remember, you wrote the article, so you can do whatever you want with it.

Finally, you also have the option of reselling your articles. You can create your own website where the articles are listed for sale. This is a great option if you can devote time to writing keyword articles on a wide range of topics or if you can hire an outsourced writer to help.

There are also online marketplaces where you can post your articles for sale. This approach is easy and convenient, but watch for high fees, as they can cut into your profits.

So, which approach is best for you? It depends. Do you already have a website or blog online? If so, add your articles to your website.

Reader love fresh content and it helps to keep them coming back. Submitting articles that you wrote to online directories is a nice way to generate traffic for your website or blog. While you do not get paid for using them, the traffic generated can create income for you. As for how you make money, it depends on whether you are selling a product or relying on advisements.

Revenue sharing websites are okay, but only if you wrote the articles yourself. Many people in your shoes would rely on outsourcing. If so, double check all outsourced articles. In fact, you should do this regardless of your intended use. Make sure the articles are truly unique.

In terms of revenue sharing websites, some will ban you if you display plagiarized content, even if you did not know it was obtained illegally. In fact, that leads to an important point.

If you are given the opportunity to choose between writing your own articles and outsourcing them, doing the work yourself is best.

Outsourced articles are nice, but your name and reputation are put online. Make sure all articles are written with quality and uniqueness.

Some Tips to Get Your Articles Read

There are many people who dread having to write papers or articles. Many just feel like it seems to be too much work and it all just goes to waste when no one reads the.

To some people, reading articles seems like work to, especially if the article is boring and very bland. Well, articles are supposed to be read, that is their purpose to impart your message and information. If it is not read, then it is waste of time and effort.

But all the same, articles have to be written to be read. It is just a matter of making them good.

Making a really good article does not have to be strenuous and straining. There are just some points needed to be reminded of, and some guides to follow. Once you get hang of it, writing articles could be fun, as well as profitable for you and your site.

Of course, writing articles must be about something you know about, that is why if you own a site, you probably are knowledgeable about that certain topic and theme. When you write about it, you will not have a hard time because you already know what it is, what it is about. It is just a matter of making your articles creative and interesting.

To make sure that your articles get read and enjoyed, here are 6 red hot tips to get your articles read. These tips will make your articles readable and interesting.

1. Use short paragraphs. When the paragraph is very long, the words get jumbled in the mind of the reader just looking at it can get quite confusing and too much of a hard work to read.

2. Reader will just quickly disregard paragraph and move on too much easier reading articles are good to look at as well as read. Paragraphs can be a single sentence, sometimes even a single word!

3. Make use of numbers or bullets. As each point is stressed out, numbers, bullets can quickly make the point easy to remember and digest. As each point, tip, guide, or method is started with a bullet or point, readers will know that this is where tips start and getting stressed.

4. Format you bullet, numbers with indentations so that your4 article will not look like a single block of square paragraphs. Add a little bit of flair and pizzazz to your articles shape.

5. Use Sub-headings to sub-divide paragraphs in the page. Doing this will break each point into sections but still would be incorporated into one whole article. It would also be easy for the reader to move on from one point to another; the transition would be smooth and easy. You will never lose your readers attention as well as the point and direction to where the article is pointing.

Provide a good attention-grabbing title or/and header. If title can entice a person's curiosity, you are already halfway in getting a person to read your article. Use statements, questions that utilize keywords that people are looking for. Provide titles or headers that describe your articles content but should also be short and concise. Use titles like, "Tips on making her want you more", or "How to make her swoon and blush". You could also use the titles that can command people, for example, "Make her yours in six easy Ways". These types of titles reach out to a persons' emotions, makes them interested.

6. Keep them interested from the start to the finish. From your opening paragraph, use real life situations that can be adopted by the reader. Use good descriptions and metaphors to drive in your point, just do not overdo it. Driving examples with graphic metaphors and similes would make it easy for them to imagine what you are talking about. Making experience pleasurable and enjoyable for them.

7. Utilize figures when necessary and not just ordinary, and insipid statements. Using the specific facts and figures can heighten your article because it makes it authoritative. But do not make it too formal, it should be light and easy in them and flow. Like a friendly teach her having a little chat with an eager student.

The Mechanics of Article Marketing

Article marketing is a very cost-efficient way of getting people to visit your site in the hopes that they will your product or service.

In fact, there are many sites these days where you can post your articles, and this is how things work. Keep in mind most websites have already posted what topics they are looking for. So, before you submit your article, check if your work is relevant to what is being asked for.

Most websites set guidelines as to the kind of articles that can be submitted. This may include a maximum number of words, that the article is original and not copied from someone else's work, must have proper English grammar and so forth. Again, read the fine print before you submit your articles.

Some sites that you submit may reserve the right to edit your content while others do not. If this is their prerogative, there may be some changes to what you wrote and there is nothing you can do about it.

You do not get paid for any of the articles you post on the website because article marketing in essence is a free form of advertising and exposure.

The best thing you can get from submitting articles is that people will know about you and the product you are selling as you have a resource box at the bottom of the page which people can click after reading the article. The resource box includes your name, website address, contact number and email.

If the article you wrote is no longer relevant, this may be pulled out so there is space for the other writers to post their own articles.

This is the reason why you should review your articles regularly so you can add new information to keep up with the times.

So how do you publish an article? Most websites will require you to sign up and become a member. Do not worry because this is free; you are simply filling up the form to create an account with them.

For writers who are just starting out, you will probably be allowed to submit ten articles first. Your article will then be reviewed by their panel of writers to check if the articles' authenticity. This may take a day or two but not longer than a week.

If this was original, then you will be notified by email that your article has been accepted. Should the allotted time pass and you have not received any word from there whether article was approved or not, send them an email to follow up the status of your pending article. If you are able to submit 10 articles and want to submit more, you have to express your intent to do and once approved, you will be able to send as many as you want as long as you continue to follow the guidelines that were set.

How things work in article marketing is very simple. You write an article based on a topic of your interest and then post it in a site that wants information pertaining to it.

You may not be compensated for hard work you put into writing the article, but you can be rewarded in other ways especially if this creates more traffic to your site.

Writing Articles and Making Money from Them

Are you looking for ways to make money online or from home?

If so, you may come across article writing online. There are a number of different ways for you to make money writing articles.

Although writing articles can help you make money from home, it is not necessarily something that you should do on a whim. First, create a small business plan. If you want to write some articles for money, you are essentially creating a business. That business needs to be well thought-out to be profitable. It is also a good idea to decide what type of articles you want to write, ahead of time.

Are you knowledgeable on subject of computers, cell phones, and software? If so, did you know you can specialize in technical writing, which tends to pay more?

Do you want to stick with writing traditional web content, or would you like to branch out to sales letters and press releases? To make the most money, you may want to consider trying all of these avenues of making money writing articles.

Next, you will want to decide who you want to write for. Do you want to write for yourself or for others? Know that each has its own advantages and disadvantages. For example, if you use your articles to create a website that will make money through advertisements, it can take up to a year or more for you to start seeing a profit. On the other hand, if you obtain clients, you should be paid within 14 days, on average.

You should also stop and think about how much money you want to make writing articles. Since you are able to write articles and work from home, you may be seeing huge dollar signs. With said, like any other work-at-home opportunity, you will not get rich right away. Web content articles vary greatly. Some writers charge $5 per page, while others can charge as much as $50 for a page.

Determining your rate ahead of time is not required, but it will help to ensure that you are paid what you are worth. Yes, you can raise or increase your rates, depending on the projects in question, but do not undersell yourself just to find a client who will pay you to write articles. After all, you want to make money, not lose it right? At the very least, make sure you are making your state's minimum wage.

If you opt to write articles for others, you will want to target either webmasters or SEO companies.

Webmasters often look for article writers for content for their websites. SEO companies are hired by webmasters to market their sites and increase their search engine rankings.

Article writing is an important component of search engine ranking.

Aside from outright targeting these individuals and companies, you can look for freelance job boards, visit freelance bidding websites, or create your own website. If you opt to write your own articles, it is important to know that you have a number of different moneymaking options. One of the easiest ways is to sell your content online. There are websites that allow you to do so, but these websites tend to take a percentage of the sale. There are also websites that either pay you outright or with a page view bonus for displaying your article on their website. Another approach that you can take is to create your own website. You can use your articles to create a content filled website. For example, if you wrote articles on dog grooming, your website could have a generalized dog care theme.

Later on, you can add additional content, such as articles that outline tips for choosing a vet and so forth. With this approach, you can make money through advertisements.

As you can see, there are a number of different ways that you can make money writing articles. In fact, that is what is so nice about doing so.

You have the freedom to decide how you want to make money.

The Fast Way to Write Articles

Are you looking to make money by writing articles? If you are, you may be curious how you make the most money. Of course, you can find well-paying content writing jobs, but there is another approach you can take.

That approach is writing articles quickly, as you are able to make more money. On that same note, you must still be able to provide quality content.

So, how can you write quality articles, but at a relatively fast pace? For starters, give it time. If you are just getting started with freelance web content writing, it may take you a few weeks or even a couple of months to get into the "grove," of things. After time, you will learn numerous tips and techniques that can improve your speed, while still allowing you to maintain the same quality.

Another way that you can write quality articles quickly is to opt for projects that are on subjects that you already know about. This can significantly cut down on your research time. Do you enjoy exercising or do you have a passion for pets? Try finding writing jobs or write your own articles on these topics.

Next, it is important to reduce distractions. For example, do you find the internet to be a distraction? If so, temporarily disable it from your computer. This will prevent you from surfing the internet when you should be writing instead. Eliminating distractions will help to keep you working at a steady pace, which should allow you to write articles at a quicker rate of speed.

One problem that plagues writers is that of writer's block. As previously stated, reducing, or eliminating distractions is advised, but an outline can also help. Before you start writing, open up a blank copy of Microsoft Word or grab a notebook.

Write down the main points that you want to cover in each article. Creating an outline is nice, as it allows you to spend more time writing and less time thinking about what you want to write. As it was previously stated, Microsoft Words is a great tool for writers. Although your clients may provide you with a form to submit your articles through or you may have another writing program on your computer, Microsoft Word is recommended.

They have a nice spell check program, which you should rely on.

Instead of going back and fixing your errors right away, let Microsoft do the work for you. Once your article is completed, you can simply go back and change the errors, which should be underlined in red for you. On that same note, be sure to proofread your article still.

Speaking of proofreading, if you are writing a series of articles, like 3 or more, you may want to write as many articles as possible and proofread when you are finished.

This may help to reduce writer's blocks. If you get "in the zone," with writing, you may not want to stop. You may find yourself writing a number of articles at a very fast rate of speed. However, if you stop to proofread each article, your flow may be disrupted. As an important note, many writers assume that the quickest way to write articles is to rewrite articles they find online. It is a gray area. If you are writing articles for someone else, your client may ask for unique articles. If so, it is okay to use the internet to research, but not to copy an article. However, some clients will ask for article rewrites. As highlighted above, there are a number of ways that you can learn to write articles at a quicker rate of speed. Although this will allow you to make more money, as you can write more articles, never underestimate the power of quality content. In fact, most clients will prefer quality content over content that can be produced in a rush.

Using Article Marketing for Your Business

One of the most incredible strategies ever to be incorporated with online advertising is article marketing. It has proven to be the most cost-efficient and most effective of them.

By the term itself, you probably would know what this kind of marketing is about. By writing articles that are content-rich, you will be able to reach more people online. Not only that, but you will also be able to project a credible image to those who may have chanced upon your articles.

With the internet now reaching world-wide market, there is a higher possibility of you getting the attention and interest of potential customers. This is what article marketing can do.

If you have not been using this in your business, you are missing more than you know. How does article marketing work?

Here is a guided tour on the step-by-step process of article marketing that will guide you on your way to achieving the kind of articles needed for your kind of business. To start with, you need to premium a quality, informative and 300 minimum word article about a certain topic related to your business.

For example, if your business is about family living, you can write an article that delves on how to spend more quality time with families.

Never write about something that is not even closely related to your niche.

After you have content written, you can now include a resource box at the end of the article. The resource box is basically a brief summary about you, your business and with a link that goes right to your website. Putting a link to your site in the resource box would is making it possible for many people who would get to read your article. This could essentially result to a large amount of new traffic to your site.

Then it is time to submit your articles to as many article directories you can find. Over the Internet, you can find various article directory sites.

There are paid and free sites.

If you are on a budget, you may opt for the free submissions being offered. But if you have money set aside for your article marketing, paying for the submission sites is also a wise move.

Whenever somebody reads your article displayed on directories, the link that leads to your site is prominent enough for readers to be able to check them out once they find your article interesting.

This way, there is a big probability of you gaining more customers whenever find what they are looking for in your site. There is also a chance that your article would get picked up by a printed publication, and the readership of the same would get to know the products or services which your business offers.

You should know that article directories are being displayed on various websites. They are seen by millions of people all over the world. This apparent visibility also makes it easier for search engines to index them.

Technique behind article marketing is back linking. Back links are links to your websites that you have somehow displayed on sites with higher page ranks. To put it simply, your site is basically sharing instant success with the sites you are linking to.

Getting indeed by search engines can be a long and trying process. Oftentimes, the result takes days or months before being acknowledged.

There are even cases where, after waiting for a long time, the result you will be getting is not the one you expected. This is the main reason why Internet marketers have resorted to back linking. You cannot get this instant online recognition in the shortest of time and without too much effort anywhere else.

You can always hire a ghost-writer to write your articles for you if you cannot write your own articles or do not have the time for them. The price rate for writing articles is from 3 to 10 dollars.

With all the advantages being presented by article writing, there is no doubt why this has become one of the most often used the Internet marketing strategy. Try to do some article marketing for your site and see the positive results it will bring to your site.

6 Red Hot Tips to Get Your Articles Read

There are many people who dread having to write papers or articles. Many just feel like it seems to be too much work and it all just goes to waste when no one reads the. To some people, reading articles seems like work to, especially if the article is boring and very bland. Well, articles are supposed to be read, that is their purpose to impart your message and information. If it is not read, then it is a waste of time and effort.

But all the same, articles have to be written to be read. It is just a matter of making them good.

Making a good article does not have to be strenuous, straining. There are just some points needed to be reminded of, and some guides to follow. Once you get the hang of it, writing articles could be fun, as well as profitable for you and your site. Of course, writing articles must be about something you know about, that's why if you own a site, you probably is knowledgeable about that certain topic and theme. When you write about it, you will not have a hard time because you already know what it is and what it is about.

It is just a matter of making your articles creative and interesting. To make sure that your articles get read and enjoyed, here are six red hot tips to get your articles read. These tips will make your articles readable and interesting.

1. Use short paragraphs.

When the paragraph is very long, words get jumbled in the mind of the reader just looking at it can get quite confusing and too much of a hard work to read. The reader will just quickly disregard paragraph and move on too much easier reading articles that are good to look at as well as read. Paragraphs can be a single sentence, sometimes even a single word!

2. Make use of numbers or bullets

As each point is stressed out, numbers and bullets can quickly make the point easy to remember and digest. As each point, tip, guide, or method is started with a bullet or point, readers will know that this is where the tips start and getting stressed. Format you bullet and numbers with indentations so that your4 article won't look like a single block of square paragraphs. Add a little bit of flair and pizzazz to your articles shape.

3. Use Sub-headings to sub-divide your paragraphs in the page.

Doing this will break each point into sections but still would be incorporated into one whole article. It would also be easy for the reader to move on from one point to another; transition would be smooth and easy. You will never lose your readers attention as well as the point and direction to where the article is pointing.

4. Provide a good attention-grabbing title or header.

If your title can entice a person's curiosity, you're already halfway in getting a person to read your article. Use statements and questions that utilize keywords that people are looking for. Provide titles or headers that describe your articles content but should also be short and concise.

Use titles like, "Tips on making her want you more", or "How to make her swoon and blush".

You could use titles that can command people, for example, "Make her yours in 6 easy Ways". These types of titles reach out to a persons' emotions and makes them interested.

5. Keep them interested from the start to the finish.

From your opening paragraph, use real life situations that can be adopted by the reader. Use good descriptions and metaphors to drive in your point, just do not overdo it. Driving your examples with graphic metaphors and similes would make it easy for them to imagine what you are talking about. Making the experience pleasurable and enjoyable for them.

6. Utilize figures when necessary and not just ordinary and insipid statements.

Using specific facts and figures can heighten your article because it makes it authoritative. But do not make it too formal, it should be light and easy in them and flow. Like a friendly teac her having a little chat with an eager student.

4 Things ALL Articles Must Have – Do not Forget!

The importance of articles in today's websites and internet-based companies are immeasurable. They dictate a lot in the success and the drive of traffic into one's site.

It has become a key element in making a site work and earns a profit. A website operator and owner must have the good sense to include articles in his or her site that will work for them and earn them the many benefits articles can give to their site.

Articles have been known to be the driving force in driving traffic to a website. Articles are a factor in giving site high rankings in search result pages. The higher a site ranks the bigger slice of the traffic flow pie he gets. With a huge number in traffic flow, there are more profits and more potential for other income generating schemes as well. But it is not just about stuffing your site with articles; they have certain requirements as well.

These requirements must be met to obtain maximum benefits an article will provide for your site. A well written article will catch the eyes and interest of your customers and keep them coming back for more.

They would also be able to recommend your site to others. Here are some tips to help you and assist you in making your articles. Below you will read about four things all articles must have to make it successful and helpful in making your site a profit earning and traffic overflowing site.

•1. Keywords and Keyword Phrases.

An article must always be centred on the keywords and keyword phrases. As each website visitor goes to a site, there are those who are just merely browsing, but actually looking for a specific something. When this happens, a searcher usually goes to a search engine and types in the keywords they are looking for (e.g., Toyota Camry, Meningitis, Tax Lawyer and Etcetera). It could be anything they want.

The Important thing is that you have an article that has the keywords that are related to your site. For example, if you maintain an auto parts site, you must be able t have articles about cars and their parts. There are many tools on the internet that provides service in helping a webmaster out in determining what keywords and keyword phrases are mostly sought out. You can use this tool to determine what keywords to use and write about.

2. Keyword Density

Know that you have your keywords and keyword phrases, you must use them fully. An article must have good keyword density for a search engine to "feel" its presence. Articles should at least have ten to fifteen percent of keyword density in their content for search engines to rank a site high in their search results. Getting a high rank is what articles do best for a site.

Keyword density is the number of times a keyword or keyword phrase is used on an article. Number varies depending on the number of words used in an article.

An effective article must have a keyword density that is not too high or too low. With a very high density, the essence of the article is lost and may turn off a reader as well as the search engines. It comes off as overeager. A low number may be ignored by the search engines.

3. Good Article Content

Like what is stated above, you cannot just riddle an article with keywords. They must also be regarded as good reading materials. Articles must be able to entertain people as well as provide good information, help for their needs. Articles should be written well with correct spelling and a good grammar. If you want people to trust you, make your work good and well thought out.

People respond well to figures, facts, and statistics. Try to get great information and as many facts as you can. A good and well written article will boost your reputation as an expert in your chosen field or topic. As more people believe in you. They will be able to trust you and your products.

4. Linking Articles

And another important thing to remember. If you are going to submit articles to ezines and/or contribute your articles to newsletters and other sites, DON'T ever forget to include a link to your site. A little resource box with a brief description of your site and you should always be placed right after your articles that you have submitted. If people like your articles, they will most likely click on the link directing them to your site.

5 Easy Ways to Get Your Creative Juices Going

Writing an article does not just mean putting down thoughts into words then typing and writing it. You have to capture the interest of your readers and get them to keep on reading. To send your message across you have to get the attention of the reader and have a firm grasp of their interest and pique their curiosity.

The main ingredient in baking up an article is a large dose of creativity. While creativity may come natural to many people, some just gets into a block or something to that effect that can drive someone crazy. Many writers have literally torn their hair out when they get writers block and just cannot seem to get their creative juices flowing.

Putting words into images in the readers mind is an art. A clear and crisp depiction requires a certain flair that only creativity can provide. Similes and metaphors help a lot, but the way an article gets entwined word for word, sentence by sentence then paragraph by paragraph into a whole article develops the essence of the article.

So just what do you have to do when nothing comes to mind? There are no sure-fire ways to get perfect ideas but there are easy ways to get your creative juices flowing. No one can guarantee you of having the perfect mindset, but many methods may aid you in achieving that state of mind. Here are five easy ways for that.

1. Keep a diary or a journal with you always.

Ideas can be triggered by anything you may hear, see, or smell. Your senses are your radar in finding great ideas. Write all of them into a journal and keep it with you for future reference. You may also write down anything that you have read or heard, someone's ideas could be used to develop your own ideas, and this is not stealing. Remember that ideas and creativity can come from anywhere; it is development of the idea that makes it unique.

2. Relax and take time to sort things out.

A jumbled mind cannot create any space for new ideas. Everyone must have a clear mind if one wishes to have their creativity in full speed. Get rid of all obstacles that can be a hindrance to your creativity. If you are bothered by something, you cannot force your mind to stay focused. Try to relax every time that you can and think about your experiences and interactions with others. Your experiences are what shape your mindset and your opinions which could be reflected on your writings. Try to discover yourself, find out what triggers your emotions. Discover what inspires you and what ticks you off. You can use these emotions to help you in expressing yourself and your ideas, with this you can grow creatively.

3. Create a working place that can inspire your creativeness.

Your working place can be quite a hindrance if it does not make you feel happy or relaxed.

Creativity comes from being in a good state of mind and a messed-up workplace that causes distraction will not be conducive in firing up your creative flow.

Surround your working place with objects that makes you happy and relaxed. You may put up pictures, scents, objects that inspire, or anything that can get your creativeness cranking. A clean, well-organized workplace also rids of distractions and unwanted hindrances. With a good working place, you can work in peace and never notice the time pass by.

4. Set the mood

Setting the mood requires you to just go with the moment or to induce yourself to feeling what makes your mind works best. Finding out what makes you tick could help you find ways to get your creative juices flowing. Set the pace and tempo for your mood and everything else will follow.

There are many ways to set the mood. Some writers have been known to use alcohol, a little sip of wine to stir up the imagination. Some would like some mood music while others let the lighting of the environment create the mood.

5. Go on a getaway and just do something unlike crazy.

Letting yourself go and have fun produces adrenaline that can make your imagination go wild. Take an adventure or a solemn hike.

Whatever it is that is unusual from your daily routine can take the rut out of your schedule. In no time at all, your creativeness will make use of that experience and get your imagination to go on overdrive.

The easiest Way to Create Articles – Public Domain!

There are many webmasters that find writing articles for their site to be a very tedious task.

Many people who need to write articles also procrastinate as much as they can to delay amount of writing they need to do. Many people dread writing articles because they find researching for the topic and writing down original materials will be too taxing on them.

You need to have your creative juices flowing and simply downloading an article would be plagiarism or tantamount to stealing, not exactly. Have you ever heard about public domain? These are articles written down by many authors that have declared their works to be public domain, which means anybody can use it for whatever purpose they want.

While most authors would prefer to copyright their work for their rights, there are also a number who does not mind sharing their work. Public domain articles are not owned by anybody and can be used and abused by anyone. The writers have waived their rights to their works, and it is out there for the public to make use of.

You can use public domain articles in helping you write your articles. With public domain articles, you can simply edit them to your own style and rewrite them as you please to make it suitable for your needs. All the ideas are there already, and it is just a matter of finding the write article with the topic or subject you need.

This is probably the easiest way to write articles. You do not need to scour around the library or the internet for hours for information and start an article from scratch.

For webmasters who are looking for articles to fill their site and to generate a high ranking for their website in search engine results, they can just modify the article by infusing keywords and keyword phrases related to their site.

A webmaster or website operator do not risk any chance of getting sued for copyright infringement because they are public domain, once again meaning that anybody can use it. Writing articles by using public domain will not require as much work as writing one from scratch would. You save a lot of time also.

One good factor in using public domain articles for your site or for any project is that you save a lot of money. You dismiss the need to hire experienced and seasoned writers that some website operators use to write their articles.

While a single five hundred worded articles would only set you down 10 to 15 dollars, this cost will drastically increase when you need hundreds of articles to fill the needs of your site.

For those who needs articles to generate newsletters or an e-zine, public domain articles will be very beneficial. You do not need to count on your contributors or pay writers to write down articles for your newsletter or e-zine. You can fill all the pages without any cost or the worry of being sued and sought after by the writers. You can simply copy the articles and place them on your newsletter and e-zine.

Public domain articles are a virtual untapped resource that many people fail to realize the true value. The power of articles, keywords, keyword phrases have been deemed invaluable these past few years for many internet-based businesses and sites want to rank high in search engine results.

The number of article and content writers have grown significantly due to the rise in demand for articles.

As newer and newer topics and subjects have arisen, there are many demands for new articles to be written. An industry has been formed and this is a worldwide demand.

Public domain articles have given a great alternative for those who are cash strapped as well as do not have the time nor the skills to do their articles for themselves.

Searching for public domain articles is as easy as 1 – 2 – 3. You can search for them in search engines and do searches in many directories for the topic or subject that you need. Read them and simply copy paste them to a word processing program and simply edit them to suit your needs.

Top Writers Around the World will write for you – outsourcing

The content of your site tells a whole lot about your website. They will basically describe what your site is about and also tell people what your site has to offer. Articles and website content makes a whole lot of difference in your site because they can catch the attention of your website visitors and keep them in there.

With good website content you get the benefit of clearly depicting what it is you want to share with people. Also, good content and articles can lead people to your site. With more traffic, you get to earn more from your site making it profitable. A sites success, be it for profit or not, is the number of the flow of traffic in your site.

So how does good content and great articles get you traffic? Well, many search engines rely on the keyword and keyword phrases of a site to put it in their results list. If your content contains a good number of keywords and keywords phrases, it may be chosen to be a part of the top listed sites in the search result pages.

But before you think of just plastering your site with all the keywords and keyword phrases it could hold, search engines also filter out that abuse. You must have good well written articles that incorporate the keywords and keyword phrases properly in their content and articles.

There are many of those who cannot afford the time to write their own website contents and articles.

While writing content articles specifically designed for internet may take some getting used to and some researching and learning, there are many writers that can be found all over the world who could do it for you.

Many of us do not have the time to learn web content writing and article writing designed for the internet. There are writers who have great experience in doing this and charge only a minimal fee for such work. Writers like this can be regarded as experts in this style of writing and can greatly help your website to get that coveted spot in the search engine rankings.

Other than getting your site in the web results page of search engines, they can also provide your site with meaningful articles, content that can impress your website visitors and entice others to view your site. Every website could use the extra traffic website visitors could invite.

Then there are those who need papers to be done either for their school or office work. Top writers around the world are very knowledgeable and do extreme researching to get a job done right. They are also very adept in many writing styles that are needed to best suit the client's need.

Many writers around the world charge a minimal fee depending on the type of writing job needed and the number of words needed in the content. Usually, a two hundred fifty worded article would cost from 4 to 8 dollars depending on the writers experience and ability. This is a small price to pay for having a content rich site or for a well-researched and written paper.

There are also many sites that can offer you these services with their team of well trained and experienced writers. They offer many writing services to cover any writing needs. A writer can be based anywhere in world and are guaranteed to offer good contents and articles. Each one is doubly checked, edited, and proofread so that you would get your money's worth.

Finding a good writer or a site that offers these kinds of services is simply done by searching for them in search engines. Type down your keyword or keyword phrase (e.g., Content Writers, Article

Writers) and you will see a long list of sites that offer these services.

The top sites would probably be the best since they have done a good job of keeping their content at a high quality to get them high rankings. But you may also want to shop around and read some of their sample work to get an idea of how much it will cost you.

Writing the Resource Box so it Makes People click

The internet is the information highway, this phrase has been used so may time it should be nominated for the Internet Cliché Award. People that go to the internet are subdivided into groups, but generally, they are out to search information. Whether for gaming, business, fun or anything else the internet has provided us with information that has proved to be very beneficial.

Through the recent years many people have learned the secrets of Search Engine Optimization.

More and more sites have seen the effects articles have done for the traffic of their sites. Some have even created sites devoted entirely to providing articles that could be read by their website visitors and have links that could lead to many sites that are related to topics and subjects of the articles.

For example, the sites may feature many articles about a whole lot of topics. As a website visitor reads the articles they have searched for, they can find at the end of the article a resource box that can be clicked on to link them to the site that has submitted the article. Of course, the article would be in relation to the site. Let's say if the article is about rotating the tires, the resource box may lead to a link to a site that sells tires or car parts.

A resource box is what you usually find at the end of an article. They will contain the name of the author, a brief description of the author, a brief description of the sponsoring site and a link. If a reader likes what they read, they will have the tendency to find out where the article came from to read more. The resource bow will be their link to the source of article, and this will entice them to go to site and do some more reading or research for the subject or topic they are interested in.

But like the article itself, the resource box must also be eye-catching to demand the attention and interest of the reader. While the resource bow encompasses only a small space, providing the right keywords and content for your resource box will provide more prodding for the reader to go to your site.

Now we know what resource boxes are, what are the benefits of having a good resource box? Mainly its driving traffic to your site. Many sites would allow articles to be placed in their sites because they can make use of the articles to fill their pages. They also get affiliation with other sites that can be beneficial for them as well. For the sponsoring site, when you get people to click on your resource box, you generate traffic that can be counted upon as potential customers.

So, what would be a good content for your resource box? Basically, it is keywords, learning about the proper keywords that people are mainly searching for. There are many tools you can find on the internet that can help you in determining what keywords to use.

Resource boxes can also make use of all the creativity it can get. You only get a small space for your resource box, so you better make the most of it. Try to catch the attention of your reader with resource box content that can make them give a second look. Unlike TV ads, you do not have visual aids to drive your point in. But you do have the power of imagination of a reader. With the right content, you can make them think and intrigued.

Another tip is to use keywords that should be related to your site. Do not mislead your potential website visitors. Build your credibility so more people would get enticed to visit your site and browse what you have to offer. Make the people click your resource box by providing resource box content that makes a lasting impression. You only get one chance to wow them and hundreds of chances to repulse them.

Never underestimate the power of resource box. It may be small in size, but they will provide a significant aid in driving traffic to your site. A boring resource box will never get a job done. Be fun and creative but at the same time show that you have a great deal to offer, too much to ask for something that could not fit a paragraph? Yes and no, there are many tips and guides that can help you in doing this, the first step is realizing how important a resource box could be in making people click your link and be directed to your site.

Effectively Using Overture/Yahoo To Get Website Visitors

Overture or now known as Yahoo because of Yahoo's takeover, was the original inventor of the use of the P4P or Pay for Performance. Overture saw that the internet was fast becoming the easiest and most convenient way to shop, and advertising was going to hit at an all-time high because of the many businesses in the arena.

To get a person to go to a site than others, it needs to be very visible. Providing ads that could direct potential consumers and costumers to their site would allow them to have an increase in traffic as well as sales. Yahoo provides a service that can put a site or company's ad in their sites that can be shown when certain keywords are inputted.

Yahoo offers a chance for any company to increase their traffic by using their services. With more people being aware of your site, there would be more traffic and visitors to your site given the chance to view your pages as well as your products.

With even a small percentage of successful sales, with a high traffic volume this could still be a substantial figure for your company. Getting a consistent substantial flow of website visitors is every company's goal. Many methods are devised and utilized to ensure that there would be more people to boost the sales and to be aware of the existence of such a product or a service. Website visitors are potentially the life blood of your internet-based business.

Yahoo/Overture utilizes the same principle as Google's Adwords. In fact, they are very similar to each other that they use keyword and keyword phrase searches and to determine which ads to show per search. When a person types in a keyword or keyword phrase to search for anything, the search engines give out the results in a page. Then at the right side of the page, you will see selected ads have paid for their ads to be viewed with certain keywords, keyword phrases searched.

For example, let us say you run a car parts retail/wholesale site. You choose keywords that can prompt or trigger your ads to be shown in the page when a keyword is searched. When a search engine user types in Honda Accord, your ad may come up if you have designated that as one of your keywords. You do not need to fully optimize your site with Search Engine Optimization methods and techniques.

While some labour so hard to make their site one of the high-ranking sites per keyword search, you get the chance to be on the top of the list or at least in the first page of a search result increasing your chance to be clicked on. With that, you drive traffic and website visitors to your site a lot faster.

You will have to pony up some cash when using this service though. There are different ways Yahoo/Overture will charge you. It may be in the number of Keywords or Keyword phrases your ad uses or in the many times your ad is clicked on. Others offer many other services like having your ad show up not only in the search engine pages but also with some third-party sites.

Third party sites support ads that have the same theme or niche as them. With more areas your ad is shown, you increase chances of people knowing about your site or product.

With more website visitors you increase the sales of your site which makes your investment with your ads a wise one.

With so many competitions on the internet-based businesses, it is necessary to take a huge leap forward from the pack by advertising. Yahoo/Overture will be a great place to start. Many have utilized their services and have reaped the rewards of this decision. It is a marketing strategy that will increase your website visitors as well as increase your sales resulting to profit.

It takes money to make money, while there are some methods that are basically low cost or free, using a marketing service such as what Yahoo and Overture offers will provide results faster and on a larger scale. Many businesses have learned this the hard way, do not be counted with them.

Here's Why Paying for Your Traffic Is A Smart Move

There are so many success stories you will hear about businesses making it good on the internet. The troubling thing is, there are maybe a tenfold or even a hundredfold of stories contradictory to theirs. Many have unsuccessfully launched the business enterprise that is internet based but only a handful shall succeed.

Is this through luck? That is even more remote. It takes good business sense and a lot of help and team effort. Most importantly, it is the eagerness to succeed and the determination to learn and the willingness to invest in a lot of hard work and some money.

The Very Basic

Like Neo, traffic is "The One". Without traffic, all your effort would just go to waste. Every business need customer, without them you would not have anyone to sell your products to. In the internet world traffic is the walk-in customer. The more traffic you have the more people would be able to sell your products to.

But like any business that is in every corner building or in the mall, not everyone that goes in will buy, but the greater of number that do come in to browse your merchandise, greater number of people that will buy your products. It is a simple and known fact.

But how do you get traffic, traffic large enough that could make a small percentage of eventual buyers enough to make a good profit. Many big companies generate traffic of tens of thousands a day and a measly ten to fifteen percent actually buys, but that small percentage is enough to provide them with good business.

Many of these success stories get their traffic from paying others. Yes, that is right; you have to spend money to make money. Advertising is key. The more people that know that your site exists;

the more people would of course go to your site, that's common sense.

While there are many ways that can get you advertising for free, this do not generate the same high volume as those methods that are getting paid. The paid advertisements include advertising schemes by Google and Yahoo.

The Value of Searches

The search and will be the easiest and fastest medium in finding what a person needs on the internet. Search engines have been very popular because they provide a vital service to many people. They are free and easy to use. With this popularity, they get many visitors and clicks that they are the most common sites that people go to. It is easy to understand why so many companies would pay to advertise with these search engines.

Search engines provide information to the millions of users that they have each day. They provide links to many sites that a user may be looking for.

If your sites link pop up in the high ranks of the search results page, you get a great chance that they will go to your site. While search engine optimization is a cheaper and low-cost way to get your site a high rank, paying for advertisements will ensure that you will be on the top ranks.

When you pay for your advertisements, it is like paying for your traffic. This may sound like not such a good idea, but the payoffs would tell a different story. When you pay for your traffic, you are guaranteed of a consistent traffic flow to your site. You will never go with an empty sales day.

Paying for your Traffic

Usually, you will be charged with the number of hits a link gets when your ads are clicked, this is called pay per click. For some search engines, you will be charged with the number of times your ad shows up when a certain keyword or keyword phrase is searched. It is imperative that you have good keyword content in your ad. There are many tools that aid you in using the right keyword for the right moment.

All the money you spend in paying for your traffic will not be for naught. You will get an impressive boost in traffic which will also result to a great boost in your sales figures. Paying for your traffic would be a really good idea and you will get all the benefits it has to offer.

How to Generate Traffic Using Only Free Methods

Putting up a company would of course require a lot of things, to get straight to the point, you need a capital. To make money requires money as well.

But of course, with the versatility internet offers, there are many ways you could find that could help optimize the potential of your site or business in generating traffic.

While there are ways to jumpstart your traffic flows, many sites do not have the resources that others have to generate more traffic for your site. Well, you do not have to spend a cent; all you need is the proper mindset and a lot of eagerness. You also must have the drive and perseverance to do hard work and research to generate more traffic for your site.

How sweet it is to have more traffic for your site without spending a single cent. Now it is a sure thing that many sites have articles that offer tips and guidelines in how to generate traffic using only free methods. Because it is possible, you do not need to speed a single cent, it may take time, to say honestly, I am not going to beat around the bush with you. You get better chances by paying for your advertisements, but at least you get a fighting chance with some of these free methods I am about to tell you.

Take advantage of online forums and online communities. The great thing about forums and online communities is that you can target a certain group that fits the certain demographic that you are looking for. You can discuss about lots of things about the niche that you represent or offer.

Another great advantage is that you know what you are getting into and you will be prepared.

With online communities, forums, you can build a reputation for your company. Show them what you are made of and wow them with your range of expertise about the subject, with that you can build a reputation and build trust with the people in your expertise and knowledge. You can also make use of newsletters.

Provide people with a catalogue of your products and interesting and entertaining articles. If you make it really interesting and entertaining, more people will sign up for your newsletter and recommend it to other people. The more people who sign up for your newsletter, the more people there will be that will go to your site increasing your traffic.

Another great idea is trading links with other sites. You do not have to spend a cent. All you have to do is reach an agreement with another webmaster. With exchanging links, the efforts both sites do will benefit both sites. Every traffic that goes to the site could potentially click on the link of your site and visit your site as well. This works well especially when both sites feature the same niche.

Write articles that could pique the attention of people that have interest in your product. Try writing articles that will provide tips and guides to other aficionados. Writing articles that provide good service and knowledge to other people would provide the necessary mileage your traffic flow needs.

Many sites offer free submission and posting of your articles. When people find interest in your articles, they have a good chance of following the track by finding out where the article originated.

Include a link or a brief description of your company with article, there is a great probability that they will go to your site. Write good content for your site. Many search engines track down the keywords and keyword phrase your site uses and how they are used. It is not a requirement that a content should be done by a professional content writer. You could do you are on, but you have to make content for your site that is entertaining as well as informational. It should provide certain requirements as well as great quality.

Generally, internet users use search engines to find what they are looking for. Search engines in return use keyword searching in aiding their search results. With the right keywords, you could get high rankings in search engine results without the costs.

All of these methods and more will drive more traffic to your site for free. All it takes is a bit of effort and extended man hours. Learn all you can about the methods depicted here and you will soon have a site with a great traffic flow without the usual costs that come with it.

How To Monetize Your Traffic So You Get The Most Out Of It

Establishing your own E-commerce site is not like what it used to be. There are thousands of competitions that is all too willing to get a bigger share of the pie. Every scheme and method you can find to augment your sales would be very beneficial.

We have got to admit to ourselves. Most of us are into it for the money. We are not going to waste our time and effort just for the fun of it. Many sites would not wait until hell freezes over just to see their profits. While there are some who takes things lightly there are always those who would rather see profit any given day.

It is common knowledge that without traffic we have no business. Like any business, without any customers you do not get sales. Traffic represents all the people that gets a chance to see what you have to offer. The more people who see your products the more people there would be to buy them.

Nobody puts up an E-commerce site that does not expect profit. We have a start-up capital that needs to be regained. With a consistent traffic, we at least have a fighting chance to achieve that probability.

Monetizing your traffic would optimize your chances of making the best out of it.

Making Money out of your Traffic

The best and most proven method of making a profit out of your traffic is using advertising. The internet generates hundreds of thousands upon hundreds of thousands of traffic every day. Most of them are searching for something. While some are just looking for information there is also a good percentage that is looking for something that they need.

The internet has proven to be a very reliable source in finding what was deemed to be a very unsearchable product. The internet has made the world a smaller place; you can advertise a product from the depths of Istanbul and still find a buyer from the centre of Philadelphia.

Generating traffic is not an easy task. You have to contend with a great number of sites to generate a good number of traffic flow. But if done successfully this could open up a Pandora's Box of possibilities. One of the benefits is monetizing your traffic flow.

So, to get to the core of it the more traffic you generate the more likely you are considered as a desirable, desirable, in a sense that a good traffic flowing site is easily convertible to profit. Basically, traffic equals profit. Advertising is the name of the game; with the good advertising scheme you can use your traffic flow to your advantage.

When you have good traffic, you have a good number of potential customers, customers that are willing to pour money into your coffers. Other than that, these are also traffic that can be redirected to sponsored links that are willing to pay you for a sizeable portion of traffic that you have generated.

This scheme is called "pay-per-click". With every click a visitor of your site makes on an advertised link you will be paid. The more traffic you generate and the more clicks that happens would spell to more profits.

Affiliate Programs

Another method of monetizing your traffic are affiliate programs. You can link up with other tried and tested sites and online companies and monetize your traffic by having a percentage of sales generated by traffic coming from your site.

The basic idea is traffic generated from your site will go to another site that can offer a product that you do not carry. Many programs can keep track and make records of transactions that was made possible because of site linkage.

When purchases are made by customers that was led by your site to their site you get a percentage of that sale. Affiliate programs would give you the benefit of monetizing your traffic without the actual need of carrying or promoting a certain product.

There are so many ways and methods to monetize your traffic. All it takes is a bit of hard work and the desire to successfully launch a profit-earning site.

The internet is a veritable source of information, many tips and guides are offered everywhere in how to monetize your traffic and make your site a good profit earner.

How To Use A Tell A Friend Script To Drive Traffic Today

More and more webmasters have recurring dilemma on how to increase the flow of traffic in the websites. During the past few years, many methods been developed to solve this predicament. While most of them would work there are those that would not make even a small impact.

One of the methods that have spawned many success stories in driving traffic into websites is viral marketing. Viral marketing makes use of the tendency of a person to share something to find informative, entertaining, or amazing.

Many companies bank on this behaviour to spread their products and increase the popularity of their company or their website. Viral marketing makes use of many mediums in enticing this behaviour. It might be in the form of an interesting story, an addicting flash game, an amusing video and many others that may catch a person's fancy.

This ingenious form of marketing is typically low cost and is a wonderful tool for any company to utilize. The benefit greatly overshadows the cost or efforts to initialize this marketing scheme. Any website would greatly benefit viral marketing.

Tell A Friend Script

One of the easiest methods in viral marketing is using a tell a friend script. It is a very simple programming script that you can attach to the programming of your website. Generally, tell a friends script are installed in pages where a media is placed so that a person can easily send the media to any of his friends or his family members.

The basic concept of a tell a friend script is a script wherein a person may input his name, e-mail address, the recipient's e-mail address and send the media to the intended recipient much like an e-mail with an attachment. As the recipient receives the e-mail, he would not think of the mail a spam mail because he would see the sender's name as someone he or she knows and trust.

Tell a friend script eliminates greatly the chances of being blocked because they use the information inputted by the sender. This allows for wider spreading of this marketing method. It can be quite sneaky, but it is very effective.

With the e-mail sent and opened the sent media will either be read, viewed, or played. Also, along with the mail would be a brief description of the company or site that sponsors the media sent. This allows for the introduction of either the site, company name or its products. The along with it is another tell a friend script.

Then the process begins again. As more people use the tell a friend script, more and more people will know of the existence of the sponsoring company or site. People who read the ads inside the mail who liked what they see would go and click on the link and visit the site. This drives traffic into site resulting to great number of potential customers.

Tell A Friend Script Availability

A tell a friend script is very simple and does not require a complicated method of programming. In fact, you can copy paste a script and simply put it on an intended page. Finding one is even simpler. All you have to do is go to a search engine and type in the search box "tell a friend script" then press enter or click go.

In the search results page, you will see many links that will direct you to a site where you can get a tell a friend script. It would just be a simple matter of looking and searching for the script and copying it to your intended web page.

With a tell a friend script viral marketing strategy you can drive traffic into your site which could potentially spell profits. This is a simple harmless script that offers great benefits for low cost paired with great creativity and foresight.

It is imperative that you have patience in using a tell a friend script. If your chosen media does not get the mileage that is expected of it, it may take some time before it gets spread or shared. But surely many people will see your ads and there is great probability that they will visit your site increasing your traffic flow.

7 Sure-fire Ways to Increase Your Traffic Starting Yesterday

Internet. Business. Profit. To fully integrate all of these words into a successful merging you will need another word. Traffic. Every article you will find about making your site or company successful would always include the importance of generating traffic.

So, we all know that in the core of it all, traffic is the most essential thing to a successful internet-based business company. Aside from ensuring that you have a great product to sell, and you have your company's internal organization well taken care of, it would be time to get to the nitty gritty of things, generating traffic.

If you already have a site and you want think that you are not getting traffic you are supposed to be getting, then it is time to reconsider. If you are contending in these very competitive businesses, you should be a step ahead of your competition, increasing your traffic flow should have been done starting yesterday.

Timing is essential, that is an old adage known to everyone. But with generating traffic, you should always be on your toes and be a day ahead of everyone. Never think of today and tomorrow as a starting point for making your site traffic laden, it should always have been yesterday.

To help you out in generating more traffic for your site, here are some seven sure-fire ways to increase your traffic starting from yesterday.

1) Invest in good advertising with search engines

Google's Adwords, Yahoo's Overture provide great advertising schemes are very truly popular and assures great traffic.

Although with this sure-fire way to increase your traffic would cost some money. While some would shy away from spending money to increase traffic, it is imperative in this case to do so because

Adwords and Overture is the top sure-fire way to increase your traffic.

You could see for yourself the success this search engine advertising methods have reaped rewards for so many companies. Lots of site feature these advertising systems and many have signed on to reap benefits. Do not be left behind. Every penny is worth it with using Google, Yahoo's advertising.

2) Exchange or Trade Links with other sites

With exchanging links with other sites, both of you will benefit from the efforts both of you do to enhance your sites traffic. When one site features another sites link, they could provide one another with the traffic one site generates. The efforts are doubly beneficial because it would seem like both of you are working to generate more traffic. The more links traded with more sites the more traffic could be expected.

3) Use Viral Marketing

Viral marketing allows you to spread the word about your company and product without any costs or if ever low costs only. This is a marketing method that can be quite sneaky; you can attach your company's name, product, or link to a certain media such as a funny video, entertaining game, an interesting article or a gossip or buzz. With this method, people get infected with the creativity and entertainment of the medium that they will pass it on too many people.

4) Search and use proper keywords or keyword phrases for your sites content

Search engines look for certain keywords that they would show in their results page. In doing so, having the right keyword and keyword phrase is a high requirement in ranking in high in search engine results. You could write your own content, or you could hire someone to do it for you.

5) Write Articles that can lead traffic to your site

Submit articles to sites that would contain the same subject that your site deals in. If you sell car parts write press releases and articles about cars and car parts. Attach your sites description and services at the end of the article as well as the link.

6) Join forums and form online communities

Capture a market and show your expertise and credibility. When you found a good foundation for your site, people will trust you and your site and will pass on too many people their trust.

Traffic will certainly increase because they know that you can provide what they need.

7) Lastly, Offer newsletters.

If many people know what you are about and your existence is shared with many others, you will find a loyal traffic that can provide you with more traffic by recommendation. If you arouse the curiosity of your customers, they would be pushed to help you with your traffic.

CPSIA information can be obtained
at www.ICGtesting.com
Printed in the USA
BVHW081231050421
604209BV00015B/1478